HISTORY & GEOGRAPHY

ISLAND COUNTRIES

Introduction |3

1. Cuba 4
Islands of the Earth |5
Pearl of the Antilles |10
Cuban History |14
Life in Cuba |18
Self Test 1 |24

2. Iceland 27
Fire and Ice |28
Saga of Iceland |32
Icelandic Life |36
Self Test 2 |41

3. Japan 44
The Islands of Japan |45
The Empire of Japan |50
Nippon |56
Self Test 3 |66

LIFEPAC Test |Pull-out

Author:
Theresa K. Buskey, B.A., J.D.

Editor:
Alan Christopherson, M.S.

Assistant Editor:
Annette M. Walker, B.S.

Media Credits:
Page 3: © hwanganator, iStock, Thinkstock; **4:** © Maria Pavlova, iStock, Thinkstock; **6:** © Quaser, iStock, Thinkstock; © mapichai16, iStock, Thinkstock; **7:** © Robert Ford, iStock, Thinkstock; **9:** © Dmitry Saparov, iStock, Thinkstock; **12:** © terex, iStock, Thinkstock; **13:** © fatchoi, iStock, Thinkstock; **15:** © Photos.com, Thinkstock; **16:** © Konstik, iStock, Thinkstock; **17:** © yelo34, iStock, Thinkstock; **19:** © Ingram Publishing, Thinkstock; **20:** zorandimazr, iStock, Thinkstock; **22:** ©Zoonar, Thinkstock; **27:** © Surangaw, iStock, Thinkstock; **28:** © IPGGutenbergUKLtd, iStock, Thinkstock; **31:** © agustavop, iStock, Thinkstock; **33:** © Jupiterimages, liquidlibrary, Thinkstock; **35:** © Isaac Ruiz Santana, iStock, Thinkstock; **36:** © topdeq, iStock, Thinkstock; **37:** © Barbara Helgason, iStock, Thinkstock; © Tyler Olson, Hemera, Thinkstock; **39:** © Susanne Erhardt, Hemera, Thinkstock; © Netta07, iStock, Thinkstock; **44:** © Supparuj, iStock, Thinkstock; **46:** © sukrita, iStock, Thinkstock; **49:** © jackiewang, iStock, Thinkstock; **51:** © Volodymyr Krasyuk, iStock, Thinkstock; **52:** © Photos.com, Thinkstock; ©Thinkstock; **54:** © U.S. Navy; **55:** © Nikola Nikolovski, iStock , Thinkstock; **57:** © scanrail, iStock, Thinkstock; **58:** © tassapon, iStock, Thinkstock; **59:** © Digital Vision., Photodisk, Thinkstock; **60:** © mykeyruna, iStock, Thinkstock; © Ryan McVay, Digital Vision, Thinkstock; **61:** © OneO2, iStock, Thinkstock; **62:** © Brand X Pictures, Stockbyte, Thinkstock; **63:** © DAJ, Thinkstock; **28:** ©Thinkstock.

Alpha Omega
PUBLICATIONS

**804 N. 2nd Ave. E.
Rock Rapids, IA 51246-1759**

ISLAND COUNTRIES

In this **LIFEPAC®** you will learn about the major archipelagos and seas of the world. You will learn how people live in these island regions of the world. You will see how the ocean waters help them earn their living and how the ocean shaped their history.

Objectives

Read these objectives. The objectives tell you what you will be able to do when you have successfully completed this LIFEPAC. Each section will list according to the numbers below what objectives will be met in that section. When you have finished this LIFEPAC, you should be able to:

1. Name and describe the different kinds of islands.
2. Locate some of the major islands of the world on a map.
3. Locate Cuba on a map and name the waters around it.
4. Describe the geography, history, industries, people, and government of Cuba.
5. Tell a little about communism and how it affects Cuba.
6. Locate Iceland on a map and name the waters around it.
7. Describe the geography, history, industries, people, language, and literature of Iceland.
8. Locate Japan on the map and name the waters around it.
9. Describe the geography, history, industries, people, art, and customs of Japan.

1. CUBA

Islands are created in many different ways. In this section of the LIFEPAC you will learn about the different kinds of islands. You will also learn about islands all over the world. You will use some of the vocabulary you learned about oceans, seas, and islands.

South and east of North America is the island of Cuba in the West Indies. These islands are part of North America because they are so close to that continent. You will learn about the island of Cuba in this section. You will learn about its geography, history, and people.

Objectives

Review these objectives. When you have completed this section, you should be able to:

1. Name and describe the different kinds of islands.
2. Locate some of the major islands of the world on a map.
3. Locate Cuba on a map and name the waters around it.
4. Describe the geography, history, industries, people, and government of Cuba.

Vocabulary

Study these new words. Learning the meanings of these words is a good study habit and will improve your understanding of this LIFEPAC.

blockade (blo′ kād). The blocking of a place by an army or navy to control who or what goes into or out of it.

coral reef (kôr′ əl rēf). A narrow ridge at or near the surface of the water made up of the skeletons of tiny sea animals.

lava (lä′ və). The hot, melted rock flowing from a volcano.

moderate (mod′ ə rāt). To make or become less extreme or violent

persecute (pėr sə kyüt). To treat badly, especially because of one's beliefs.

ration (rash′ ən). To allow only a certain amount; to limit.

rhythm (riŦH′ əm). Any movement with a regular repetition of a beat, accent, rise and fall, or the like.

slogan (slō′ gun). A word or phrase used by a group to advertise its purpose.

volcano (vol kā′ nō). A crack in the earth where lava comes out.

Note: *All vocabulary words in this LIFEPAC appear in* **boldface** *print the first time they are used. If you are unsure of the meaning when you are reading, study the definitions given.*

Pronunciation Key: hat, āge, cãre, fär; let, ēqual, tėrm; it, īce; hot, ōpen, ôrder; oil; out; cup, put, rüle; child; long; thin; /ŦH/ for then; /zh/ for measure; /u/ or /ə/ represents /a/ in about, /e/ in taken, /i/ in pencil, /o/ in lemon, and /u/ in circus.

Islands of the Earth

All land on earth is surrounded by water. The seven largest pieces of land we call *continents*. The thousands of smaller bits of land are called *islands*. A clustered group or string of these islands is called an *archipelago*. A very small island is called an *islet* (i′ lit).

There are two main types of islands: those that are part of a continent and those that are out in the oceans, far away from any land. Islands of the continents often used to be part of the land. Something happened to separate the island from the continent. The British Isles in Europe are a good example. Long ago, the islands were a peninsula attached to Europe. Over time the land sank and the ocean opened a strait, the English Channel, between the island of Great Britain and Europe.

Islands which form in the oceans are often made by **volcanoes**. Volcanoes are mountains made when the super-hot, melted rock from the center of the earth escapes to the surface through a crack. The liquid rock squirts out, cools, becomes hard, piles up, and forms a mountain. Many of these mountains are made on the bottom of the ocean. If they get tall enough to stick out of the water, they become islands. The islands of Japan and Hawaii were made this way.

People have actually been able to watch an island being born from a volcano. In 1963 scientists noticed steam and **lava** coming out of the ocean near Iceland in Europe. By 1967 the volcano had built an island that was over a square mile in size. It was named Surtsey.

There are a few other ways that islands can be created. One is by the build-up of a **coral reef**. Corals are small sea animals that live inside hard shell-like skeletons. Corals live in groups, and when they die their hard skeletons pile up, forming a reef. Sometimes the coral gets tall enough to come out of the water and make an island.

| An atoll

One very unusual and pretty type of coral island is called an *atoll* (a' tôl). An atoll is created when a coral reef forms around an island that sinks over many years. After the land is gone, the reef continues to grow until it becomes an atoll, an island shaped like a doughnut. The ocean in the middle of the circle of land is called a *lagoon*.

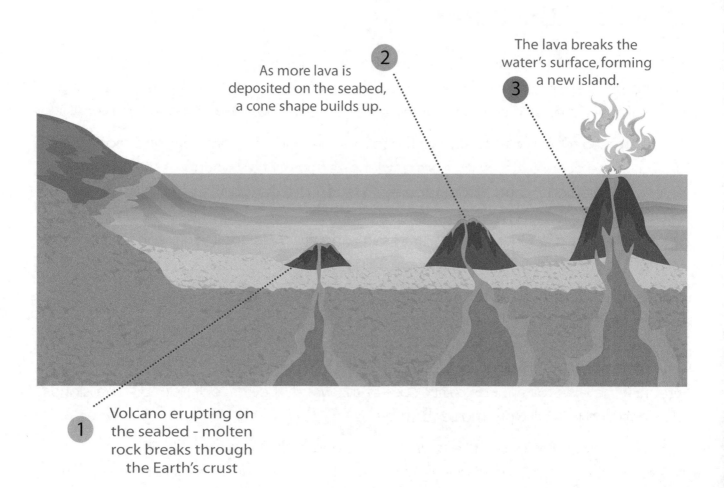

2 As more lava is deposited on the seabed, a cone shape builds up.

The lava breaks the water's surface, forming a new island.
3

1 Volcano erupting on the seabed - molten rock breaks through the Earth's crust

| Volcanic island

Another type of island is formed when the ocean or a river piles up dirt in one spot. *Barrier islands* are made by waves and currents piling up dirt in the ocean beside the coast. Assateague Island National Seashore is a barrier island off the coast of Maryland. It has beautiful beaches and is home to herds of wild ponies.

| A river delta lagoon

Islands are also sometimes created in river deltas. As the river goes into the ocean, it leaves dirt that piles up and makes islands that the river goes around on both sides. There are many islands like this in southern Louisiana. They are at the mouth of the Mississippi River where it flows into the Gulf of Mexico.

Match each word with the correct description.

1.1	_____ volcano	a. water in the center of an atoll
1.2	_____ islet	b. a group of islands
1.3	_____ lagoon	c. one of the seven largest pieces of land on earth
1.4	_____ archipelago	d. a very small island
1.5	_____ continent	e. where lava comes out of the earth

Match these items.

1.6	_____ Hawaii	a. barrier island
1.7	_____ Great Britain	b. separated from the continent
1.8	_____ atoll	c. created in a river delta
1.9	_____ Assateague	d. built by coral reef
1.10	_____ Gulf islands of southern Louisiana	e. created by a volcano

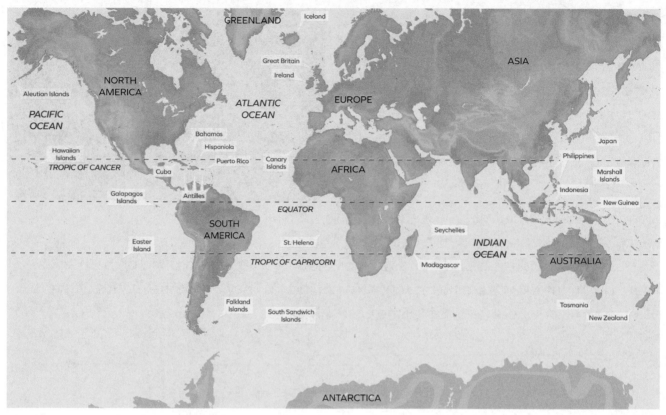

| Islands and archipelagos of the world

 Map Work. Remember, on most maps north is up, south is down, east is right, and west is left.

1.11 Put north, south, east, or west in each blank.

a. The Hawaiian Islands are _____ of the Marshalls. (Consider the shortest distance.)

b. Japan is _____ of the Philippines.

c. The Canary Islands are _____ of Africa.

d. St. Helena is _____ of Iceland.

1.12 Which continent is closest to these islands?

a. The Bahamas _____ b. New Zealand _____

c. Madagascar _____ d. Philippines _____

e. Galapagos _____ f. Ireland _____

g. Falkland _____ h. St. Helena _____

i. Seychelles _____

Islands come in all sizes. The largest island is Greenland. It covers 840,000 square miles (2,175,600 square kilometers) in the North Atlantic. That is larger than Alaska and California put together! The smallest islets are often just rocks poking up above the waves.

There are many countries in the world that are on islands. We will be studying the island countries of Cuba, Iceland, and Japan in this LIFEPAC. The Philippines, Indonesia, Great Britain, and New Zealand are all nations made up only of islands. Some of these countries have hundreds or even thousands of islands. Indonesia has more than <u>13,600</u> islands!

Islands are located all over the world in every climate. The Galapagos Islands and Madagascar are warm, tropical islands near the equator. Greenland, in spite of its name, is a cold island, covered almost completely with thick ice. Some of the islands around Antarctica are buried so deep under ice that the land is never seen.

| The Galapagos Islands

It is the Europeans who mapped the earth and its many islands in the 1600-1800s. Many of the islands, however, even the ones way out in the middle of the Pacific Ocean, had people living on them long before the European explorers arrived. These people had come from the continents in canoes or boats hundreds of years before the Europeans. Sometimes by exploring and sometimes by getting lost in storms, people found the islands and made their homes there, far from the continents.

Island people must be good friends with the ocean. They must cross it to reach their neighbors. They often get most of their meat from it. They also must survive its violent storms. So the story of the island nations must include the water around them, for the ocean is part of their home and a part of their lives.

Choose the best match for each one.

1.13	_____ Iceland	a. more than 13,600 islands
1.14	_____ Greenland	b. tropical island near Africa
1.15	_____ Indonesia	c. island nation studied in this LIFEPAC
1.16	_____ Madagascar	d. largest island on earth

Write *true* or *false* on the blank.

1.17 _____ Islands are only found near the equator.

1.18 _____ Island people usually stay away from the ocean.

1.19 _____ Many people lived on islands before the Europeans explored the earth.

Pearl of the Antilles

Cuba. Columbus discovered the island of Cuba on the first of his four voyages to America. Because he thought he was near India, all the islands of the area are called the West Indies. Within the West Indies are several archipelagos. Cuba is part of the Antilles Islands in North America. It is sometimes called the "Pearl of the Antilles" because of its beauty.

The country of Cuba includes the island of Cuba and many nearby smaller islands. The only other island large enough to be worth mentioning is the Isle of Youth, south of Cuba's western end. Altogether, the land in Cuba is about the same size as the state of Ohio.

Cuba is located about 90 miles (140 km) south of Florida. North of Cuba, between Cuba and Florida, are the Straits of Florida. West of Cuba, between Cuba and Mexico, is the Yucatan Channel, another strait. Yet another strait, the Windward Passage, is east of Cuba, between it and the island of Hispaniola. South of Cuba is the Caribbean Sea.

Remember, a sea is part of an ocean that is partly surrounded by land. The Caribbean Sea is a good example. Central America is the land on its west side. South America is the land on the south side. The Antilles Islands curve around to form the east and north sides. It is still part of the Atlantic Ocean, but the land around it lets geographers call it a sea as well.

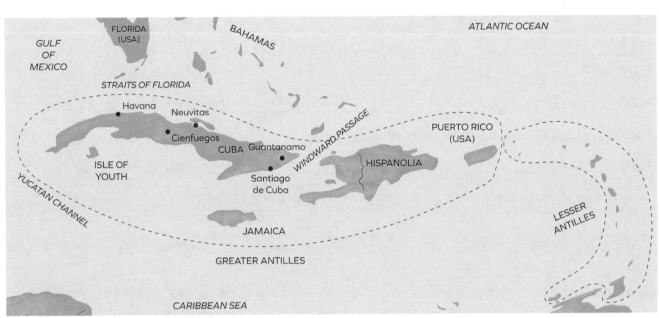

| Cuba, "Pearl of the Antilles"

 Map Work. Remember, on most maps north is up, south is down, east is right, and west is left.

1.20 Notice that the Antilles Islands north of the Caribbean are called the Greater Antilles, while the islands east of the Caribbean are called the Lesser Antilles. Why do you think they were named that way? _____

_____

_____

1.21 Using a map or a globe, circle the Gulf of Mexico on the map on this page.

1.22 Find and circle the island of Puerto Rico.

1.23 Find and circle the island of Jamaica.

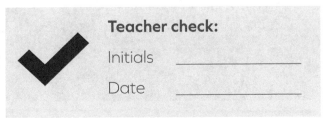
Teacher check:

Initials _____

Date _____

Complete these sentences.

1.24   All of the islands southeast of North America are called the

_____ .

1.25   The _____ is the area of water north of Cuba,

between Cuba and Florida.

1.26   The _____ is the strait west of Cuba.

1.27   The _____ is the strait east of Cuba.

1.28   The _____ is the waters south of Cuba.

1.29   Cuba is called the Pearl of the _____ .

1.30   The _____ is the large island south of

Cuba's western side that is part of the country of Cuba.

Geography. Cuba is the largest island in the West Indies. It is a lovely island with many resources. Only about one-fourth of the land is mountains or hills. Much of the land is gentle hills or plains which are good for farming or raising cattle. Cuba has fertile soil and a warm climate that makes it great for growing crops.

| Havana

Sugar is the most important crop of Cuba. Sugar cane is the largest cash crop grown in Cuba and brings in the most money. Tobacco is second. Much of the tobacco crop is made into cigars by hand. A hand-made Cuban cigar is considered by many people to be the finest in the world. Other important crops include rice, coffee, and fruit.

| Sugarcane plantation

Cuba also has many minerals. Cobalt, nickel, iron, copper, and manganese are all found on the island. Salt, petroleum, and natural gas are also found there.

The coast of Cuba has many bays and several fine harbors. Havana, the capital, is also the nation's largest port. Other harbors also have port cities. Nuevitas is another port city on the north coast. Cienfuegos, Guantánamo, and Santiago de Cuba are port cities on the south coast.

Cuba has a *semi-tropical* climate. That means that the cool ocean winds keep it from being too hot even though it is in the tropical zone. (The tropical zone is the hottest part of the earth, around the equator between the Tropic of Cancer and the Tropic of Capricorn.) The temperatures usually are around 70° F (21° C) in the winter and 80° F (27° C) in the summer. Of course, it gets cooler in the mountains because the altitude is higher.

The temperatures on any island are always affected by the ocean. Oceans tend to warm up and cool down more slowly than the land; so oceans, and the land near them, tend to stay warmer in the winter and cooler in the summer. Thus, the ocean tends to **moderate** island climates.

Cuba has a wet season and a dry season. The dry season lasts from November to April, while the wet season runs from May to October. August to October is the **hurricane** season in the Atlantic Ocean. The strong winds of a hurricane can destroy buildings and crops. The rain and waves can flood the coast and port cities.

Complete these sentences.

1.31 _____ is the most important crop in Cuba.

1.32 Cuba's second most important crop, _____ , is made into _____ by hand.

1.33 Cobalt, nickel, and iron are _____ found in Cuba.

1.34 _____ is the capital of Cuba.

1.35 The coast of Cuba has many bays and several good _____ .

1.36 Cuba has a _____ climate.

1.37 The ocean tends to _____ island climates.

1.38 December is during the _____ season in Cuba.

1.39 August to October is the _____ season.

Cuban History

Peaceful Indians were living on Cuba when Columbus discovered it in 1492. The Spanish began to send their own people to live on the island in 1511. Spain wanted to use the island as a supply base for ships going to and from the Americas.

| Flag of Cuba

The Spanish colonists set up large plantations to grow sugar and tobacco. They forced the Indians to work on their farms. Many of the Indians died from diseases and cruel treatment. So many Indians died that the colonists began to bring in slaves from Africa to do the work.

Slowly Cuba's population grew, and it began to trade with the nations around it. But Spain kept very strict control of the colony, which the colonists did not like.

Cuba was a Spanish colony until 1898. Many times during the 1800s some of the Cuban people rebelled against Spanish rule, but each time, the Spanish government would use its soldiers to kill the leaders and stop the revolt. Finally, after a large rebellion called the Ten Years War which began in 1868, the Spanish government agreed to give the Cubans more freedom. It still would not give them independence, though.

Another revolt began in 1895. By this time the United States had many businesses in Cuba. America had even tried to buy the island from Spain, but had always been refused. The American president, William McKinley, sent the battleship *Maine* to Havana to protect the Americans and their property there. In February of 1898, the *Maine* mysteriously blew up in Havana harbor. America blamed Spain and declared war.

| Theodore Roosevelt, our 26th president, was part of the Rough Riders, a fighting unit in the Spanish-American war.

The United States easily defeated Spain in the short Spanish-American War. As part of the treaty, Spain gave up all claim to Cuba. The Cuban people set up their own government by 1902, and the American army left.

The United States, however, was not willing to let the Cubans be completely independent. Part of the Cuban constitution, called the Platt Amendment, said that the United States could send its army back if it wanted to do so. The Americans used the Platt Amendment many times to send in an army to stop revolts against the new government.

After the Spanish-American War, the United States controlled Cuba. Much of the land and industry were owned by Americans. The Cuban people did not like this and often spoke out, and fought against the Americans. Eventually, in the 1930s, a **dictator** named Fulgencio Batista took control of the government. Dictators often take control when people are unhappy and revolts are common.

Batista ruled Cuba until 1959, when he was forced to leave Cuba by yet another successful revolt. The man who led that revolt became Cuba's new dictator. His name was Fidel Castro.

Write *true* or *false* on the blank.

1.40 _____ Cuba was discovered by Columbus.

1.41 _____ Cuba became a British colony.

1.42 _____ The Cuban people were happy with the Spanish government.

1.43 _____ Spain ruled Cuba until 1956.

1.44 _____ Spain lost Cuba in the Spanish-American War.

1.45 _____ The U.S. gave Cubans complete control of their own country after the Spanish-American War.

1.46 _____ Batista and Fidel Castro were both Cuban dictators.

Fidel Castro set up a communist government in Cuba. A communist government takes all the businesses and land away from the people. The government owns everything, and the people work only for the government. Communists also teach that there is no God. They often put people in prison for believing in God. Communist governments do not allow the people the freedom to choose their officials, speak freely, run their own businesses, or worship God. This is the government that Cuba has had since 1959.

After World War II (1939-1945), the United States led the free countries of the world in trying to stop communism. The many communist countries wanted to take over all the nations of the world. The United States used its power and strength to make sure that did not happen. But America has never been able to get rid of the communists in Cuba that stole all the American businesses and land there. Cuba and the United States have never trusted each other since Fidel Castro became dictator.

In 1962 the Soviet Union, the most powerful communist country, tried to put missiles in Cuba to threaten the United States. The American president

| Soviet missile on Cuban launcher

ordered the navy to **blockade** Cuba to stop the missiles from being delivered. Many people thought the Soviets and the Americans would go to war over the missiles. Instead, the two sides made an agreement. The Soviets promised not to put the missiles in Cuba, and America promised not to attack Cuba.

| Poor neighborhood in Cuba

By 1990 communism was almost completely gone in most countries. Most people realized what a poor kind of government it was and revolted against it. Only a few countries today are still communist. Cuba is one of them.

Communist countries are usually very poor, because governments do not run farms and businesses as well as individuals can. The Soviet Union used to give Cuba a great deal of money before 1990 to help keep the communist government strong. After 1991 Russia (the biggest part of the Soviet Union) stopped giving Cuba money, and Cubans soon began having serious problems. They did not have enough food, clothing, or even school supplies.

Things were so bad by 1994 that many people built boats and tried to escape from Cuba. Many came to the United States, which had always welcomed people fleeing from Fidel Castro's Cuba. But so many people were coming that President Bill Clinton refused to take them, and instead sent them back to Cuba.

Cuba is trying to give the people some land and businesses of their own to help the country survive better, but change is coming very slowly. There is still no toleration of people who speak out in opposition to official policy.

Check the statements that are true of a communist government.

1.47 _____ They are usually rich.

1.48 _____ People are not allowed to own businesses and land.

1.49 _____ The government owns everything.

1.50 _____ The government teaches people to believe in God.

1.51 _____ People choose the government officials.

1.52 _____ People are allowed to speak freely if they do not like the government.

Answer these questions.

1.53 What country led in trying to stop communism after World War II?

_____ .

1.54 What did the Soviet Union do in 1962 that made the U.S. blockade Cuba?

_____

_____

1.55 What happened to communism around 1990?

_____

_____

1.56 What help did the Soviet Union give Cuba before 1991?

_____ .

1.57 What did many of the people of Cuba do beginning in 1994 when things became so bad there?

_____

_____

Life in Cuba

The people of Cuba come from three different groups. The largest group is the descendants of the Spanish settlers who came to Cuba. The smallest group is the descendants of the black African slaves who were brought in to do the work. The middle-sized group is a mix of Spanish and African. The communist government has succeeded in seeing that the three different groups have the same opportunities and are treated alike.

Before "the Revolution" which brought Fidel Castro to power, most of the people of Cuba were Roman Catholic. Roman Catholicism is the religion of Spain and became the religion of all of her colonies. After the Revolution, the government began to **persecute** those who believed in religion. People who are Christians often are not allowed to have jobs. Believing in Jesus is a very difficult decision in Cuba, because it makes the believer's life very hard. Today only about one in three Cuban people are Roman Catholic, and only one in a hundred are Protestant.

The communist government has done a good job of giving the people a basic education. All children are required to attend school from age six to age twelve. The schooling is free. Nearly everyone can read and write.

Reading is very popular in Cuba. The people especially like to read anything that comes from outside of Cuba. The government does not like Cubans to read about life in other countries, since the government tells the people many lies about how wonderful life in Cuba is. The government does not want the people to read the truth in books and magazines from outside the country. This kind of control over what people are allowed to read is called *censorship*. It is always done in communist countries.

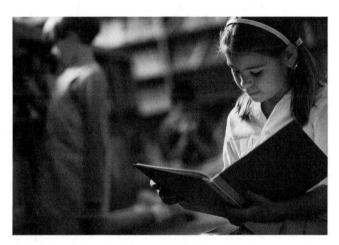

| Reading is popular in Cuba.

The people in Cuba know their government is lying, but to say so or try to change things gets people into trouble. They might even be jailed for being *counter-revolutionaries*, persons who oppose the Revolution that made Fidel Castro dictator. So most of the people say nothing and pretend to agree with the government. Every year, a few who are brave enough to ask for changes are killed or put in jail.

Communism claims to make everyone equal. In fact, the people who are important in the government get special treatment. They get better houses and food. They can shop at special stores that import well-made goods from other countries. Ordinary Cuban people get into trouble if they even try to shop at the special stores.

Most Cuban people must stand in long lines to buy everything. They wait in line at the bread store, at the milk store, and at the meat store. Many foods and goods, such as clothes or shoes, are **rationed**. For example, a person might be allowed to buy only one pair of shoes a year. This allows even the poorest people to get a share of the food and goods. However, stores will often run out of food or shoes before all the people have bought what they are allowed to buy. Communism never has enough for everyone.

Things that are made in a communist country are usually not very well-made. Shoes, for example, fall apart quickly. In the United States, if a shoe factory made poor quality shoes, no one would buy them, and the shoe factory would then go out of business. So, to stay in business, American factories work to make good shoes, fire workers that do poor work, and pay more money to their better workers.

In Cuba though, all the shoes are made in government shoe factories. No one can be fired; and since people who work better are not paid more, everyone does only the work they must do, and no one cares about doing good-quality work. So, the shoes, clothes, and other goods made in Cuba are of poor quality. They cannot be sold in other countries, because no one would buy them. This helps keep Cuba's economy poor.

Most of the farms in Cuba are owned by the government. The people who raise the crops are paid a salary. They make the same amount of money no matter how well they work or how much money is made selling the crops. A few farms in Cuba are still owned by individual people. However, these farmers are required to sell their crops to the government at whatever price the government decides to pay, so even the farmers who own their land really work for the government.

Houses and apartments are also built by the government. There are not enough of those for everyone, either. Many families must share houses or apartments. In the countryside, the people often live in houses with thatch roofs, because better housing is not available.

| Tobacco farmer

In spite of all this, Cuban people love their country. It is their home. They also love music and sports. Cuban music is very lively. Much of it comes from African and Spanish **rhythms**. Baseball, basketball, and track and field events are very popular. Even in a communist dictatorship, people still find ways to enjoy life.

Match these items.

1.58 _____ censorship

1.59 _____ counter-revolutionary

1.60 _____ Roman Catholic

1.61 _____ Spanish

1.62 _____ African

1.63 _____ mixed Spanish/African

a. largest group of people

b. religion of all Spanish colonies

c. tries to change things in Cuba

d. smallest group of people

e. not allowing people to read what they want

f. middle-sized group of people

Answer these questions.

1.64 Why aren't shoes well-made in Cuba?_____

_____

_____

1.65 Are all people equal in Cuba? Explain. _____

_____

_____

1.66 Is it easy to be a Christian in Cuba? Why or why not?_____

_____

_____

1.67 Name three of the things Cuban people enjoy. _____

_____

Fidel Castro is still the most important man in Cuba. Like many dictators, he created a *personality cult* about himself. This means that he expected the Cuban people to worship him almost as if he were a god. The newspapers had pictures of all his visits around the country. His speeches were always printed in the newspapers and broadcast on television or radio.

| Fidel Castro with rebel soldiers (1959)

People came and cheered when he spoke. Everyone was to act as if they thought he was great and wonderful. Anyone who did not like Fidel Castro, and said so, might have ended up in jail!

Fidel Castro believed that free governments should be attacked by revolutionary armies and destroyed. He thinks that all governments should be communist like his. Many, many times Cuban soldiers have been sent to other countries to help fight with communist rebels. Cuban soldiers have fought against non-communist groups in Angola, Ethiopia, and Nicaragua. Since the fall of communism in Europe however, Russia has stopped paying for these soldiers, and most have come home.

Fidel Castro expected his people to love the Revolution and to support communism no matter what. When Cuba lost the extra money from Russia, food, gasoline, and clothes became more difficult to get. Instead of trying new ways to get more, Fidel Castro told the people to do the best they could with less and be proud of their government, which would never stop being communist. **Slogans** telling people to support the Revolution are everywhere in Cuba.

Raúl Castro, Fidel's brother, assumed the office of President in a temporary transfer of power due to Fidel Castro's illness on July 31, 2006. The First Vice President assumes presidential duties upon the illness or death of the president according to the Cuban Constitution. Then on February 24, 2008 Raúl Castro was elected President at the National Assembly. This took place because Fidel Castro announced his intention not to stand for President again earlier that month. Only communists can run in the elections and Fidel was the only one who could run for president until he stepped aside for his brother. Raúl was also elected First Secretary of the Communist Party at its Sixth Congress on April 19, 2011, after having served as Second Secretary behind his brother for 46 years. Although Raúl is officially in power it is not known how this will change life for the people of Cuba.

Do this activity.

1.68 Using an atlas, globe, encyclopedia, or online resources name the continent on which each of these countries is located.

a. Angola _____

b. Ethiopia _____

c. Nicaragua _____

Complete these sentences.

1.69 _____ is still the most important man in Cuba.

1.70 Fidel Castro believes that all governments should be _____ like his.

1.71 Many times Fidel Castro sent _____ to fight for communist groups in other parts of the world.

1.72 Fidel Castro expected the Cuban people to _____ communism.

1.73 Only _____ can run for elections in Cuba.

Review the material in this section to prepare for the Self Test. The Self Test will check your understanding of this section. Any items you miss on this test will show you what areas you will need to restudy in order to prepare for the unit test.

SELF TEST 1

Choose the correct word from the list to complete each sentence (2 points each answer).

islet	volcano	lagoon	coral reef
communist	archipelago	tropical	censorship
barrier	sea		

1.01   Cuba has a _____ government.

1.02   A _____ climate is found near the equator.

1.03   A _____ is built up by the skeletons of small sea animals.

1.04   _____ prevents people from reading things the government does not want them to read.

1.05   A _____ is a mountain made when melted rock comes up from the center of the earth.

1.06   An _____ is a group of islands.

1.07   An _____ is a very small island.

1.08   A _____ is a piece of the ocean that is partly surrounded by land.

1.09   A _____ island is made when waves and currents pile up dirt beside the coast.

1.010   A _____ is the water in the center of an atoll.

Write _true_ or _false_ on the blank (1 point each answer).

1.011   _____   Cuba has many minerals.

1.012   _____   Most of the land in Cuba is mountains.

1.013   _____   Cuba has fertile soil for crops.

1.014   _____   Batista was a Cuban priest who helped the Indians.

1.015   _____   Communism encourages people to believe in God.

1.016   _____   Communist countries are usually poor.

1.017 _____ The largest group of Cuban people are of African blood.

1.018 _____ Cuba does not have enough homes for everyone.

1.019 _____ Cuban soldiers have often fought in other countries.

1.020 _____ Very few Cubans can read and write.

Match these items with the best description (2 points each answer).

1.021 _____ Hawaii   a. sea south of Cuba

1.022 _____ Great Britain   b. Maryland barrier island

1.023 _____ Greenland   c. volcanic islands

1.024 _____ Indonesia   d. island, east coast of Africa

1.025 _____ Cuba   e. island, once part of European continent

1.026 _____ Assateague National Seashore

     f. capital of Cuba

1.027 _____ Madagascar   g. island, just south of Cuba

1.028 _____ Caribbean   h. Pearl of the Antilles

1.029 _____ Havana   i. nation with over 13,600 islands

1.030 _____ Isle of Youth   j. largest island in the world

Put the correct answer on the blank (3 points each answer).

1.031 _____ was the dictator of Cuba for many years.

1.032 The continent closest to Cuba is _____ .

1.033 August to October is dangerous because it is the _____ season in the Atlantic Ocean.

1.034 _____ was the European man who discovered Cuba.

1.035 Cuba was a colony of the country of _____ for many years.

1.036 Right before the Revolution, most of the land and businesses in Cuba were owned by people from the country of _____ .

1.037 People from the continent of _____ were the first to explore and map the earth.

1.038 _____ is the largest island in the West Indies.

1.039 _____ is the most important crop in Cuba.

1.040 _____ , used to make cigars, is the second most important crop in Cuba.

Teacher check:		Initials	_____	80
Score	_____	Date	_____	100

2. ICELAND

Iceland is an island nation near the Arctic Circle, a land of both fire and ice. You will learn why in this section. You will learn about Iceland's difficult and violent history. You will also learn about the modern, free country of Iceland, its people, and its industries. Iceland is an island that uses its resources well, but will never be able to live with them in complete safety.

Objectives

Review these objectives. When you have completed this section, you should be able to:

2.   Locate some of the major islands of the world on a map.
6.   Locate Iceland on a map and name the waters around it.
7.   Describe the geography, history, industries, people, language, and literature of Iceland.

Vocabulary

Study these new words. Learning the meanings of these words is a good study habit and will improve your understanding of this LIFEPAC.

ash (ash). What remains of a thing after it has been thoroughly burned.

chieftains (chēf' tan). The head of a clan or group; leader.

diatomite (dī at' ə mīt). A chalk-like rock used for filtering, as an abrasive, as a filler in explosives, and for insulation.

fjord also **fiord** (fyôrd). A long, narrow bay bordered by steep cliffs.

geyser (gī' zer). A spring that sends up fountains or jets of hot water or steam.

hydroelectric (hī ' drō i lek' trik). Producing electricity by using the power of moving water.

manuscript (man' yu skript). A handwritten or typewritten book or article.

pagan (pā ' gun). One who worships many gods or no god; heathen.

pollution (pə lü' shun). The dirtying of any part of an environment, especially with waste material.

Pronunciation Key: hat, āge, cãre, fär; let, ēqual, tėrm; it, īce; hot, ōpen, ôrder; oil; out; cup, put, rüle; child; long; thin; /ŦH/ for then; /zh/ for measure; /u/ or /ə/ represents /a/ in about, /e/ in taken, /i/ in pencil, /o/ in lemon, and /u/ in circus.

Fire and Ice

Iceland is an island in the North Atlantic that is part of Europe. It is just south of the Arctic Circle (a few places on the north coast cross the circle) in an area that often has earthquakes. Its closest neighbor is Greenland, in North America. That island is 180 miles (290 km) west and north of Iceland. The Denmark Strait separates the two islands. North of Iceland is the Greenland Sea, but all the rest of the water around the island is simply the Atlantic Ocean.

| Flag of Iceland

In spite of its name, Iceland is not an island of ice. In fact, most of the island is covered with tundra-like grasses and mosses with a few stunted trees. There are several large glaciers in the interior (center) of the island, including Vatnajökull, the largest glacier in Europe. Iceland, like Cuba, is both an island and a country that includes nearby smaller islands. The Westmann Islands to the south are the only ones you need to know. The town of Vestmannaeyjar is on Heimaey, the largest of those islands. The capital of Iceland is Reykjavík, in the southwest.

Iceland is a "land of fire." Like Japan and Hawaii, it is an island created by volcanoes. It has many volcanoes that are still active, and one or another of them erupts about every five years. One eruption in the Westmann Islands created the new island of Surtsey in 1963.

| Lava flowing through surrounding snow

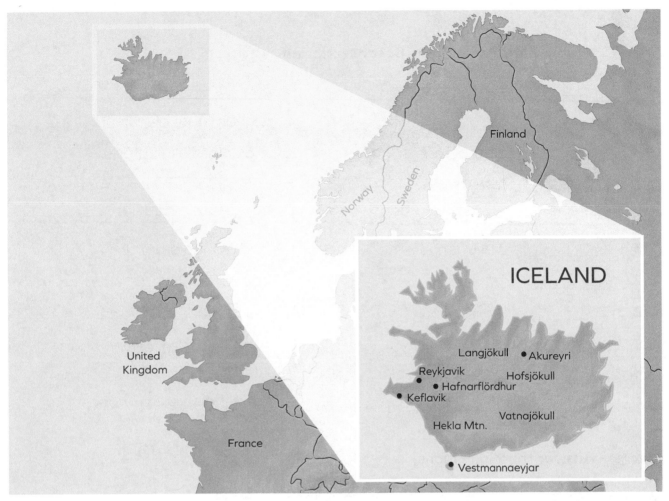

| Iceland and neighboring countries

The eruptions can be very dangerous. An eruption on Heimaey Island in 1973 forced everyone living there to leave for several months. The worst eruption was in 1783, when Lakagigar erupted. The clouds of gas and **ash** killed most of the animals and crops on the island. One of every three people in Iceland died of hunger or disease afterward. That eruption is considered by many people to have been the worst in human history. Ash from it spread all over the world.

All the heat from the Icelandic volcanoes creates hot springs and **geysers**. These are places where water inside the earth has been heated and comes to the surface. Some of these pools of water are hot enough to cook eggs! In fact, we get the word "geyser" from a hot springs named "Geysir" in Iceland that sprays water up 196 ft (60 m) into the air!

The heat these springs produce is called **geothermal** energy. "Geo" refers to the earth, and "thermal" refers to heat. It is heat from the earth. The people of Iceland use it to heat their homes, buildings, and even swimming pools.

Match the word with the best description.

2.1	_____ Greenland	a.	town on the island of Heimaey
2.2	_____ Iceland	b.	islands south of Iceland
2.3	_____ Vatnajökull	c.	major island in Europe
2.4	_____ Westmann	d.	major island in North America
2.5	_____ Reykjavík	e.	hot spring in Iceland, sprays water
2.6	_____ Vestmannaeyjar	f.	had a huge eruption in 1783
2.7	_____ Lakagigar	g.	capital of Iceland
2.8	_____ Geysir	h.	island made by a volcano in 1963
2.9	_____ Surtsey	i.	strait between Iceland and Greenland
2.10	_____ Denmark	j.	largest glacier in Europe

Answer these questions.

2.11   What is heat taken from the earth called? _____

What do the people of Iceland do with that heat? _____

_____

Only a little of the land in Iceland is _arable_, or good for growing crops. The arable land is found along the coast, and so are most of the cities. The coast of Iceland is very jagged. There are many peninsulas, bays, and **fjords**, especially along the north coast.

The interior is a rough, rugged, wild place. Very few people live there. It is covered with old lava fields, mountains, volcanoes, and glaciers. The major roads do not even go across the center of the island. The most important road, the Ring Road, goes all the way around the island, mostly along the coast.

The glaciers in the interior melt to create many fast-moving streams that flow out toward the ocean. These rivers and many small lakes have many kinds of fish. These streams are also used to create electricity. This type of power does not create **pollution**. Iceland has more **hydroelectric** power than it needs. The Icelandic people hope to find ways to sell the extra electricity to Europe some day.

| A fjord

Iceland has very few mineral resources. Pumice, from lava, and **diatomite** are about all that can be found there. This makes the hydroelectric power all the more important.

The climate in Iceland is not as cold as you would think, in spite of how close it is to the Arctic Circle. The Gulf Stream, an ocean current, brings warm water up from the Gulf of Mexico and the South Atlantic Ocean. This current keeps it cooler in the summer and warmer in the winter, than it would be without the Gulf Stream. On the south coast, the temperature goes down close to freezing, 32° F (0° C), in the winter, and it usually only goes up to about 52° F (11° C) in the summer. The north coast is only somewhat cooler than the south. By contrast though, central Alaska, which is at the same latitude as Iceland goes down to -60° F (-50° C) and up to 90° F (30° C).

The worst thing about the climate in Iceland is the daily weather. Rain, snow, wind, and storms are very normal. The weather often changes quickly, too. It might be sunny in the morning, stormy at noon, and sunny again by afternoon. Icelandic people joke that they don't get actual weather, just samples of different kinds of weather.

Iceland does not have sunshine <u>all</u> day in the summer—that only happens inside the Arctic Circle—but it comes very close. In the middle of the summer, the sun does set, but the night sky never gets dark enough to see the stars before it rises again. In the winter, the sun only comes up for a few hours before it sets again. Some of the towns down in the fjords do not see the sun for months, because it is blocked by the cliffs around them.

The only mammal **native** to Iceland is the arctic fox. There are, however, over seventy kinds of birds that nest on the island in the summer. Icelanders hunt many of the birds for food. The ptarmigan, an arctic bird you studied in an earlier LIFEPAC, is a favorite for winter holiday dinners. Seals and whales are often found visiting as they travel along the coast. Rats, mice, reindeer, and minks were brought in by people, and now live wild on the island.

Choose the correct letter to complete the sentence.

2.12 Iceland's arable land is found mostly _____ .
a. in the interior
b. along the coast
c. in the south
d. in the northwest

2.13 Major roads go _____ .
a. from east to west
b. out from Reykjavík
c. around, along the coast
d. across the interior

2.14 Iceland has _____ .
a. many streams for hydroelectric power
b. rich reserves of coal and oil
c. a great deal of arable land
d. a warm, tropical climate

2.15 _____ are native to Iceland.
a. Rats
b. Minks
c. Mice
d. Arctic foxes

2.16 The weather in Iceland is _____ .
a. very changeable
b. usually wet and warm
c. usually sunny and cold
d. seldom rainy or windy

Write *true* or *false* on the blank.

2.17 _____ The interior of Iceland is a rough, wild place.

2.18 _____ Pumice and diatomite are the only major minerals found in Iceland.

2.19 _____ Iceland is as cold as most places near the Arctic Circle.

2.20 _____ The sun does not set in Iceland all day in the summer.

Saga of Iceland

The people of Iceland are great writers. For many generations they have written *sagas*, or long stories, about people who lived on their island. <u>This</u> saga is about the history of Iceland.

No one lived in Iceland until about 800 years after Jesus was born. Some monks from Ireland found the island at about that time, but they did not stay. In about the year A.D. 874, the first permanent settlers arrived from Norway. They were Vikings.

Vikings were fierce warriors and sailors. They would attack towns all along the coast of Europe to steal and take the people as slaves. They were some of the best sailors of their time. The rest of Europe did not sail as far as the Vikings did until the time of Prince Henry, about 500 years later! The Vikings of Iceland even sailed to Greenland and North America.

Iceland was settled by Vikings and their slaves, taken mostly from northern Europe. They had no king, and in A.D. 930 they set up the *Althing*, a form of government similar to a parliament or congress, to govern their island. The Althing began as a meeting once or twice each year of the powerful **chieftains** on the island. Today the Althing is the world's oldest parliament.

| A Viking

Unfortunately, the **pagan** Vikings preferred fighting over obeying the Althing. They constantly killed each other over insults and murders of their own family members. The Althing decided that the whole island should become Christian in A.D. 1000, because pagans and Christians were fighting over religion, as well. Finally, the king of Norway took advantage of the fact the Icelanders were unable to work together. He took over the island in about 1264.

Iceland was ruled first by Norway, then by Denmark, until 1944. This period of time was a very difficult one for the Icelanders. The island had been covered with trees when the settlers first arrived in A.D. 874, but within a few hundred years, the trees had all been cut down. The people had no wood for boats and fires. To get sailing vessels and heat sources, the Icelanders were forced to trade with Europe; the Europeans took advantage of Iceland's need.

The kings in Denmark treated the Icelandic people very badly. They were allowed to trade only with the men the king allowed, and those men cheated them. They charged very high prices for food and goods brought in from Europe and paid very little for the fish and wool the Icelanders had to trade in return. As a result, the whole country became very poor.

It is interesting that even when they were so desperately poor, Icelanders still taught their children to read and write. In Europe at that time, reading was an unusual skill, known only to a wealthy few. In Iceland, even the Vikings had always been taught to read and write. Many great sagas about the settling of Iceland were read and written in houses of poverty.

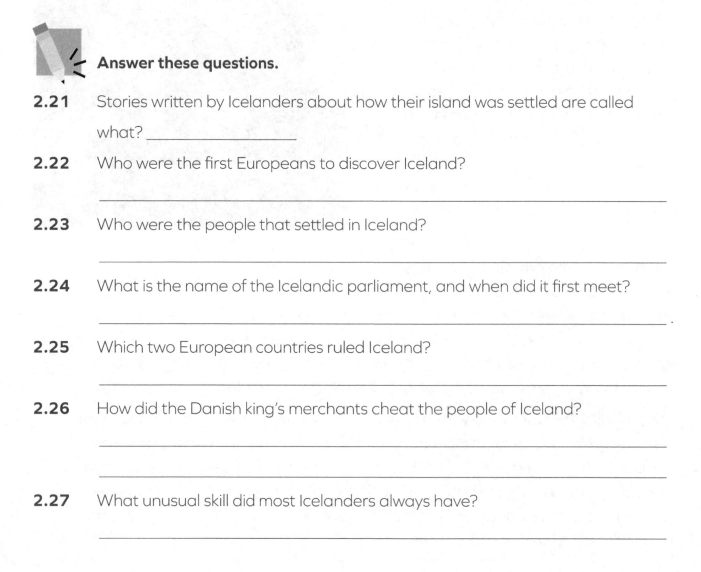

Answer these questions.

2.21   Stories written by Icelanders about how their island was settled are called what? _____

2.22   Who were the first Europeans to discover Iceland?

_____

2.23   Who were the people that settled in Iceland?

_____

2.24   What is the name of the Icelandic parliament, and when did it first meet?

_____ .

2.25   Which two European countries ruled Iceland?

_____

2.26   How did the Danish king's merchants cheat the people of Iceland?

_____

_____

2.27   What unusual skill did most Icelanders always have?

_____

HISTORY & GEOGRAPHY 408

LIFEPAC TEST

NAME _____

DATE _____

SCORE _____

80

100

Put a *C* **if the statement best describes Cuba, an** *I* **if it best describes Iceland, or a** *J* **if it is Japan** (2 points each answer).

1. _____ capital is Reykjavík

2. _____ in Asia

3. _____ Caribbean Sea is just south

4. _____ Arctic Circle touches the northern coast

5. _____ Althing has met there for over 1,000 years

6. _____ in Europe

7. _____ settled by Vikings

8. _____ took much of its culture from China

9. _____ capital is Havana

10. _____ has much good farmland and many mineral resources

11. _____ the good land is around the coast, the interior is rough and wild

12. _____ Westmann Islands are part of the country

13. _____ is part of the West Indies

14. _____ in North America

15. _____ Fidel Castro was the dictator

16. _____ was discovered by Columbus

17. _____ was never controlled by a European country

18. _____ a nation that manufacturers many kinds of goods to export

19. _____ wool and fish are traditional exports

20. _____ sugar and tobacco are important exports

Write *true* or *false* on the blank (1 point each answer).

21. _____ Cuba has a free, elected government.

22. _____ Iceland is covered almost completely with ice.

23. _____ Japan is a country with many different industries.

24. _____ About half the Cuban people are of French blood, the rest are of Indian blood.

25. _____ Iceland had a feudal government with an emperor before Spain conquered the island.

26. _____ The people of Japan love beauty in nature.

27. _____ Most of the people can read and write in all three of the countries we studied.

28. _____ Iceland publishes more books per person than any other nation on earth.

29. _____ Japan is a safe, uncrowded country with almost no natural dangers.

30. _____ Communist countries are usually very wealthy.

Explain in at least five sentences which of the three islands we have studied you would most like to live on and why (10 points this answer).

31. _____

_____

_____

_____

_____

_____

Match these items (2 points each answer).

32. _____ communist

33. _____ barrier

34. _____ saga

35. _____ geothermal

36. _____ volcano

37. _____ sea

38. _____ atoll

39. _____ samurai

40. _____ glacier

41. _____ archipelago

a. heat from the earth

b. circular coral reef island

c. a group of islands

d. the largest one in Europe is in Iceland

e. soldiers in a Japanese lord's army

f. island made near coast by currents and waves

g. government that owns all land and businesses

h. piece of an ocean partly surrounded by land

i. Icelandic story

j. a place where lava comes out of the earth

Complete the sentences using words from the list (2 points each answer).

Tokyo	Antilles	Honshu	Gulf Stream
Fuji	Youth	Madagascar	Surtsey
Nippon	Indonesia		

42. Mount _____ is the tallest mountain in Japan.

43. The _____ is an ocean current that keeps Iceland warmer than most countries at the same latitude.

44. Cuba is a part of the _____ Islands.

45. _____ is an island made in Iceland by a volcano in 1963.

46. The Isle of _____ is part of Cuba.

47. _____ is an island on the east coast of Africa.

48. _____ is the Japanese name for their country which means "source of the sun."

49. _____ is a Japanese island.

50. _____ is the capital of Japan.

51. _____ is an island nation made up of over 13,000 islands.

Life was very difficult for the Icelandic people under the Danish kings. Almost everyone on the island was a farmer. Sheep had been brought to the island by the first settlers and did well, however very few food crops would grow in the cool climate, only things like potatoes and turnips. Other than these few things, the island's only other possible export was a plentiful supply of fish that could be dried for shipping.

| Icelandic sheep

The Icelanders, therefore, had to trade wool and fish for almost every thing else they needed to live. The Danish merchants priced their imports so high that most of the Icelandic population suffered from hunger.

The hard life was made even worse by the natural disasters common to the island. Volcanic eruptions, plagues, unusually cold winters, and earthquakes killed many people. Early in the 1800s the king even refused to let the Althing meet any longer. He would not allow the people of Iceland to have any say in how they were ruled.

However, later in the 1800s, things began to change in Europe. The absolute power of kings was going away and more and more kings lost their power to parliaments and the people. Iceland never had a revolutionary war like the United States. Instead, Denmark was slowly convinced to give the Icelandic people more freedom.

In the middle of the 1800s, the Althing was allowed to meet again, although only to advise the king. Later, Iceland was allowed to trade with any nation it wanted. That freed the people from having to deal only with Denmark's dishonest merchants. Their lives began to improve as they received better prices on the goods they bought and sold.

The year 1874 was the 1000-year anniversary of the founding of Iceland. The king of Denmark, after much discussion, agreed to give the country a gift for the occasion. He gave the Althing the power to write laws and run the country, though Iceland was still not given its independence. In 1918, Iceland became an independent country but still under the Danish king. That ended in 1944, when Iceland finally became a completely independent republic.

Write *true* or *false* on the blank.

2.28 _____ Wheat and wool were Iceland's only important exports.

2.29 _____ Natural disasters made the hard life on Iceland much worse.

2.30 _____ Iceland won its independence by fighting a war.

2.31 _____ The Althing never stopped meeting in Iceland.

2.32 _____ Iceland was not allowed freedom to trade as they wanted until independence.

2.33 _____ 1918 was the 1,000-year anniversary of the founding of Iceland.

2.34 _____ Iceland became completely independent in 1944.

Icelandic Life

Industries. Today Iceland is a modern, free nation. Fishing is the most important industry. The ocean around Iceland has some of the best fishing in the world. After independence, the government spent money on better boats and factories to prepare fish to sell. Fishing and the industries that support it (boat building, shipping, etc.) are the biggest source of money for Icelanders.

| Icelandic fishing village

Iceland also has many small factories that make goods, mostly things they need on the island. There are a few factories that make things to export. Since Iceland has so much hydroelectric power, an aluminum plant was built to take advantage of the cheap power supply. Minerals are imported, made into aluminum, then exported mostly to Europe.

Iceland also makes and exports wool clothes. Icelandic sheep come in all colors, from black, to brown, to white. Their soft, natural-colored wool is made into beautiful sweaters, hats, and other clothes to be sold all over the world.

Thanks to its abundant geothermal and hydroelectric power, Iceland has very little pollution. This is very unusual for a modern nation. The lack of pollution means the fish around the island are healthier, and the island itself more beautiful. This attracts many tourists. More and more people are visiting Iceland to see volcanoes, glaciers, streams, waterfalls, and mountains that do not have a brown fog hanging around them.

| Reykjavík, Iceland

Before independence, most of the people of Iceland were farmers. Today, very few are. Eight out of every ten people in Iceland now live in a city, and most of those live in or near the capital, Reykjavík. Those who still farm, grow mostly hay, to feed their sheep and cattle during the winter. Sheep remain the most important farm animal, but more farmers are also raising chickens, pigs, and cattle.

Language and literature. The language of Iceland is almost the same as the old Norse language of the Vikings. It has changed very little in hundreds of years. Children in school today can read sagas written 700 years ago! That is impossible in English, French, or most other languages because they have changed too much. Icelandic has not changed because the people of the island had so little contact with the rest of the world until recently.

The Icelanders are proud of their ancient language. They are very careful not to use foreign words for new things. Instead, when there is a new invention, a special committee makes up an Icelandic name for it. Some of the names can be funny. For example, the word for a pager, that interrupts everything with its beeping, is *fridthjofur*, thief of peace!

| Viking rune (rocks with stories carved into them)

Icelandic museums have a large collection of priceless old **manuscripts**. Many of these are sagas about the warriors who first came to Iceland and fought among themselves over it. They were once stories that were told at night around the fire in the great halls of the Vikings. Eventually, they were written down and became a rich part of Iceland's history.

Icelanders do not have family names, like Smith or Jones. A person's last name comes from his father. For example, Eric's children take their last name from him. His son, Lief, would be Lief Eric*sson*. His daughter, Helga, would be Helga Eric*sdottir*. They just take the father's first name and add the ending for a son or daughter!

Even during the hardest times, under the Danish kings, the Icelanders were great writers and poets. Poets and writers led the movement for Icelandic independence. Writing and poetry continue to be important today. Not only does everyone go to school and learn to read, but the Icelanders also publish more books per person than any other country in the world!

Complete these sentences.

2.35 _____ is the most important industry in Iceland.

2.36 The most important animal is the _____ , raised for wool and meat.

2.37 Due to _____ and _____ power, Iceland has very little pollution.

2.38 The Icelandic language is very much like the old _____ language of the Vikings.

2.39 Many of the _____ are about the warriors who first settled Iceland.

2.40 If you were an Icelander, what would your last name be?

_____

2.41 Icelanders publish more _____ per person than any other nation.

People. The people of Iceland live very much like those in the United States. They have televisions, cell phones, cars, computers, and other modern things. They vote for their leaders and were the first nation to elect a woman president (in 1980). Most of the people belong to the Evangelical Lutheran Church, which is the official church of Iceland. Its pastors are paid by the government with money taken in taxes.

Everything in Iceland is very expensive and the taxes are very high, but Icelanders constantly buy things. Everyone works, usually very long hours, to have as much money as possible to spend on things. So prices stay high, because people still buy things in spite of the expensive prices!

Almost everyone in Iceland can swim. Every town has a large swimming pool heated by geothermal energy that can be used all year long. The people also love to ride horses. Until independence, horses and boats were the only ways to get around the island. (Iceland has no railroads.) Icelandic horses are small, sturdy animals with thick coats to keep them warm. Even though they have roads and cars, the people love to ride horses for the fun of it. Chess, card games, soccer, and tests of strength, such as weightlifting, are also popular.

| Geothermal swimming pool

Traditional Icelandic foods are fish and mutton (meat from a sheep). Ancient people also ate eggs from the birds that nest on the island, and many people still like them today.

Puffin, a wild bird found in Iceland, is a popular food. The national food, however, is *skyr*, (skir) a sour, yogurt-like dish made from milk.

Before independence, Icelanders rarely ate fresh fruit or garden vegetables. They had to be imported from other countries and were too expensive to eat regularly. Today, however, it is easier for airplanes and fast ships to bring in fresh produce. Also, the clever Icelanders have used some of their cheap geothermal energy to build hothouses. In these heated glass houses, food can be raised that wouldn't normally grow in cold Iceland.

| A Puffin

For a long time during their history, the people of Iceland suffered. Today they are proud of their success in building such a rich, modern nation. They are very proud of their past and love to talk about the heroes of their sagas. The Vikings do not fight any longer, but they live on in the sagas and the hearts of the Icelanders.

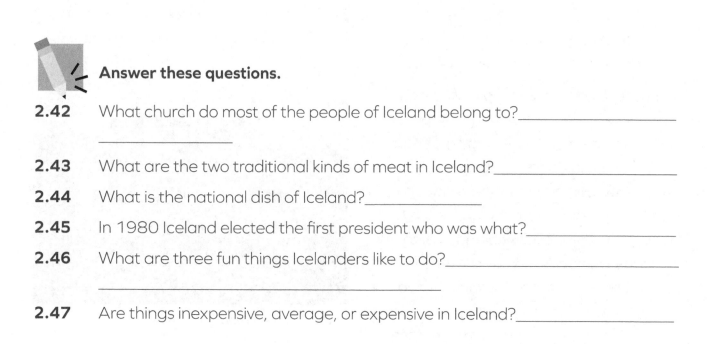

Answer these questions.

2.42   What church do most of the people of Iceland belong to?_____

_____

2.43   What are the two traditional kinds of meat in Iceland?_____

2.44   What is the national dish of Iceland?_____

2.45   In 1980 Iceland elected the first president who was what?_____

2.46   What are three fun things Icelanders like to do?_____

_____

2.47   Are things inexpensive, average, or expensive in Iceland?_____

Review the material in this section to prepare for the Self Test. The Self Test will check your understanding of this section and will review the other section. Any items you miss on this test will show you what areas you will need to restudy in order to prepare for the unit test.

SELF TEST 2

Put an *I* on the line if the word or phrase is about Iceland, a *C* if it is about Cuba, or a *B* if it is about both (each answer 2 points).

2.01 _____ part of Europe

2.02 _____ part of North America

2.03 _____ fishing is the most important industry

2.04 _____ sugar is the most important industry

2.05 _____ includes a main island and many smaller nearby islands

2.06 _____ was a Spanish colony

2.07 _____ settled by Vikings

2.08 _____ has many active volcanoes

2.09 _____ is a republic

2.010 _____ is communist

Match each item with the best description (2 points each answer).

2.011 _____ Isle of Youth

2.012 _____ Westmann

2.013 _____ Antilles

2.014 _____ Reykjavík

2.015 _____ Madagascar

2.016 _____ Caribbean

2.017 _____ Denmark

2.018 _____ Havana

2.019 _____ Surtsey

2.020 _____ Greenland

a. strait between Iceland and Greenland

b. island created by a volcano in 1963

c. Cuba's archipelago

d. capital of Cuba

e. islands just south of Iceland

f. capital of Iceland

g. sea just south of Cuba

h. island just southwest of Cuba

i. world's largest island

j. island on the east coast of Africa

Choose the correct word from the list to complete each sentence (2 points each answer).

geothermal	hydroelectric	geyser	Gulf Stream
Arctic Circle	Althing	Denmark	sagas
Skyr	Great Britain		

2.021 The _____ is an ocean current that keeps Iceland warmer than most countries at the same latitude.

2.022 _____ is an island in Europe.

2.023 Icelanders have written many _____ about the lives of the people who settled their island.

2.024 Iceland uses _____ power from its many hot springs.

2.025 _____ is a European country that ruled Iceland for many years.

2.026 The _____ is the world's oldest parliament.

2.027 Iceland's northern coast just touches the _____ .

2.028 _____ is the national dish of Iceland.

2.029 Iceland's many streams and rivers give _____ power.

2.030 A _____:_____ is a hot spring that shoots up a spray of water.

Write _true_ or _false_ on the blank (1 point each answer).

2.031 _____ Iceland's best farmland is in the center of the island.

2.032 _____ There are no glaciers in Iceland.

2.033 _____ The people of Iceland were treated badly by the European kings.

2.034 _____ The Ring Road is in Cuba, along the coast.

2.035 _____ Cuba has fertile soil.

2.036 _____ The weather in Iceland changes a great deal.

2.037 _____ The horse and the polar bear are native to Iceland.

2.038 _____ Vikings were peaceful, Christian cattle ranchers.

2.039 _____ Fish and wool are the most important exports of Cuba.

2.040 _____ Iceland does not have very much pollution.

Put the correct answer on the blank (3 points each answer).

2.041 _____ islands are a type of island created when waves and currents pile up sand and dirt along a coast.

2.042 A very tiny island is called an _____ .

2.043 The most important farm animal in Iceland is the _____ .

2.044 Cuba and Iceland are in the _____ Ocean.

2.045 _____ was the European who discovered Cuba.

2.046 _____ is the dictator of Cuba.

2.047 Icelanders publish more _____ per person than any other country on earth.

2.048 A coral reef island that is a circle with a lagoon in the center is called an _____ .

2.049 Hawaii and Japan are examples of islands made by _____ .

2.050 Which is closer to the equator, Iceland or Cuba? _____ .

Teacher check: Initials _____

Score _____ Date _____

80 / 100

3. JAPAN

Japan is not one island surrounded by many others. The country of Japan is an archipelago made up of almost 4,000 islands, but most of the people live on the four main ones you will learn about in this section. Japan, like Iceland, must deal with volcanoes and earthquakes. You will learn how Japan deals with these dangers, as well as its rich history and how it has become one of the greatest industrial nations on earth. You will also learn something about the polite, beauty-loving Japanese people.

Objectives

Review these objectives. When you have completed this section, you should be able to:

2. Locate some of the major islands of the world on a map.
8. Locate Japan on the map and name the waters around it.
9. Describe the geography, history, industries, people, art, and customs of Japan.

Vocabulary

Study these new words. Learning the meanings of these words is a good study habit and will improve your understanding of this LIFEPAC.

ally (al′ ī). A nation or group united with another for some special purpose.

atomic bomb (əu tom′ ik bom). An extremely powerful bomb.

clan (klan). A group of related families that claim to be descended from a common ancestor.

code (kōd). A collection of laws or rules.

democratic (dem ə krat′ ik). Of a government that is run by the people who live under it, or through their elected representatives.

erupt (i rupt′). Burst out or explode.

independent (in' di' pen' dənt). Thinking or acting for oneself; not influenced by others.

landlord (land' lord). A person who owns buildings or land rented to others.

meditate (med' ə tāt). To think quietly; reflect, especially about serious things.

pottery (pot' er ē). Pots, dishes, or vases made from clay and hardened by heat.

ruins (rü' inz). That which is left after a building or wall has decayed or fallen to pieces.

shrine (shrīn). A place to worship and pray.

treaty (trē' tē). A formal agreement, especially one between nations, signed and approved by each nation.

Pronunciation Key: hat, āge, cãre, fär; let, ēqual, tėrm; it, īce; hot, ōpen, ôrder; oil; out; cup, pút, rüle; child; long; thin; /ŦH/ for then; /zh/ for measure; /u/ or /ə/ represents /a/ in about, /e/ in taken, /i/ in pencil, /o/ in lemon, and /u/ in circus.

The Islands of Japan

Japan is a nation of islands that curve along the east coast of Asia. The country has four main islands: Hokkaido, Honshu, Shikoku, and Kyushu. There are also almost 4,000 smaller islands. Altogether Japan has about as much land as the state of Montana.

Most of the people and all of the large cities are on the four big islands. Honshu is the largest of the four. The capital city of Tokyo is on Honshu. This island is considered to be the Japanese homeland.

The northernmost island, Hokkaido, has the smallest population and the most farmland. The two smallest islands, Shikoku and Kyushu, are very close to the southern edge of Honshu, across a narrow strait called the Inland Sea.

Japan's closest neighbor is the peninsula of Korea which is on the other side of the Sea of Japan (called the East Sea by the Koreans) across from the main island of Honshu. The huge nation of China is west of the southern Japanese islands, across the East China Sea. North of Japan are more islands which are part of Russia in the Sea of Okhotsk. East of Japan is the Pacific Ocean.

The Japanese islands are the tops of a chain of underwater mountains that run all along the east coast of Asia. Mountains, therefore, are the main part of the land. About seven-tenths of the land is mountains. Much of that is too steep or high for people to live on and grow food. Only a small part of the land (about one out of every ten acres) is arable or good for growing crops.

The highest mountain in Japan is Mount Fuji, called Fujiyama there. It is one of many Japanese mountains made by volcanoes. Mount Fuji is widely admired in Japan for its even shape and great beauty, especially when it is capped with snow.

There are over 200 mountains in Japan that were made by volcanoes. About 36 of these are still called "active," which means that lava or gas has come from them recently. Only twenty of the volcanoes have actually **erupted** since 1900.

All of the heat from under the earth makes many hot springs. These hot springs are popular bathing places. People like to visit and relax as they soak in the hot water. There are many small businesses in Japan which offer comfortable places to enjoy the numerous hot springs.

| Hot springs

Japan is in a very dangerous part of the world. It is located in a place where many earthquakes occur. Japan may have as many as three earthquakes a day! Most of the quakes are too small to even be felt, but some of the earthquakes can be very dangerous. An earthquake near Tokyo in 1923 killed about 130,000 people.

Today, the Japanese take many precautions against earthquakes. Their buildings are made to not fall apart in a quake. Earthquake drills are held, like fire drills in America, and special teams train to help people during an emergency. Even with all that preparation, though, 6,300 people died in an earthquake near Kobe in 1995.

There is another danger from earthquakes for people near the ocean. An earthquake that is near or under the ocean causes a huge wave that can crush houses and people near the shore. These waves are so common in Japan that all over the world they are called by their Japanese name, *tsunami* (sü nä' mē).

Japan suffered its strongest ever earthquake and accompanying tsunami in March of 2011. This disaster severely devastated the northeastern part of Honshu Island. Thousands of people were killed and several nuclear power plants were damaged. The economic slowdown already taking place in the country was further amplified by the strain of this large scale catastrophe.

The Japanese Islands also are in danger from storms which are called typhoons. The word typhoon (tī fün') comes from the Chinese words *taai fung*—"great wind."

Typhoons are like hurricanes in the Atlantic. They are huge wind and rain storms that regularly hit the Japanese Islands.

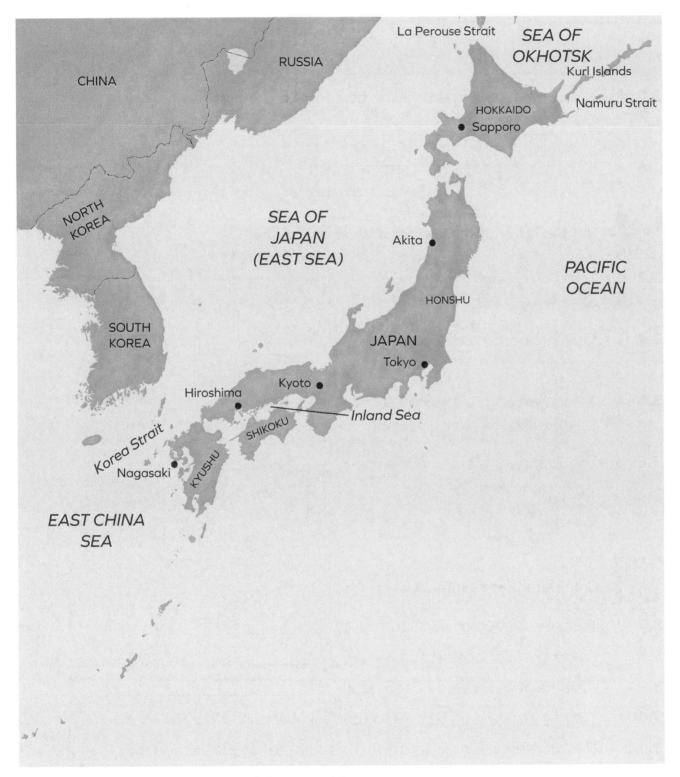

| The main islands of Japan and their neighbors

Complete these activities.

3.1   Name the four main Japanese Islands.

a. _____   b. _____

c. _____   d. _____

3.2   Name the four bodies of water that surround Japan.

a. _____   b. _____

c. _____   d. _____

Put the letter of the correct answer on the line.

3.3   There are about _____ active volcanoes in Japan.
a. 200   b. 52   c. 6   d. 36

3.4   Most of Japan is covered with _____ .
a. plains   b. mountains   c. rain forests   d. tundra

3.5   A huge wave caused by an earthquake is called a _____ .
a. typhoon   b. volcano   c. tsunami   d. surf

3.6   The Japanese Islands have small _____ almost every day.
a. earthquakes   b. volcanic eruptions
c. typhoons   d. tsunamis

Complete these sentences.

3.7   The tallest mountain in Japan is Mount _____ .

3.8   The largest Japanese Island is _____ .

3.9   Japan is about as large as the state of _____ .

3.10   _____ is the capital of Japan.

3.11   The strait between Honshu and the southern islands is called the

_____ .

The northern Japanese Islands are on the same latitude as Maine, while the southern ones are on the same latitude as Florida; so Japan's climate changes quite a bit from north to south. Hokkaido has cold, snowy winters and cool summers, while Kyushu (the southernmost island) has a warm, almost tropical climate. The climate also changes going up and down the mountains!

In addition to latitude and altitude, the ocean has an effect on the climate in Japan as well. No place on the islands is more than 100 miles from the sea, so the ocean's temperature directly affects the temperature of the land.

Two ocean currents bring very different temperatures to Japan. The Oyashio Current flows in from the north along the west coast, toward Asia. It brings cold air and heavy winter snow to that side of the islands, especially in the north.

The Japan Current comes up from the Philippine Islands to the south along the east (Pacific) coast. It warms Kyushu, Shikoku, and southern Honshu before it pushes out into the Pacific Ocean. The Japanese call this current *Kuroshio*, or "Black Current" because the water is dark-colored.

The high mountains of central Honshu, called the Japanese Alps, protect the Pacific coast from the cold wind and weather of the northwest. Most of the people and cities are on the warmer Pacific side of the islands toward the south. In fact, the Asian side of Honshu, over the Alps, is called the "backside of Japan" by the people.

| The Japanese Alps

Japan has very few natural resources. There are few minerals, and the lack of arable land makes it difficult to even grow enough food for the people. Wild plants and animals are mostly found high in the mountains, because all the flat land is used for people and crops.

Write *true* or *false* on the blank.

3.12 _____ The Pacific (east) coast is called the "backside of Japan."

3.13 _____ The Oyashio Current brings cold temperatures from the north to Japan's Asian (west) coast.

3.14 _____ The Japanese Alps are on the island of Honshu.

3.15 _____ The Oyashio Current is also called the Black Current.

3.16 _____ The Japan Current brings warm temperatures up from the south.

3.17 _____ Hokkaido has a warm, almost tropical climate.

3.18 _____ Japan has many natural resources, including many kinds of minerals.

3.19 _____ No place in Japan is more than 100 miles from the ocean.

The Empire of Japan

Japanese myths say that their islands were created by a god and goddess. They felt their creation was so beautiful that they decided to live there. Their children became the gods of Japanese religion. Some of the less important of these gods became the parents of the Japanese people.

Japanese legend says that the first emperor of Japan was the descendant of the sun goddess. He was supposed to have become emperor 660 years before the birth of Jesus. In fact, it was almost 400 years after Jesus' death that the Yamato **clan** became powerful enough to rule Japan. The emperor of Japan today is still from the Yamato clan.

The Japanese borrowed much of their culture from the powerful nation of China on the mainland of Asia. They began using Chinese writing, government organization, art, and religions. The Japanese changed these things to meet their own needs and used them to create their own empire.

| Japanese kanji symbols for America

The emperor of Japan has always come from the Yamato clan, but usually the emperor had very little power. Other clans ruled the country in the emperor's name. From A.D. 1192 to 1867, the actual ruler of Japan was a succession of soldiers called the *shogun* (general). The clans fought wars among themselves to make their leader the shogun. Some clans were able to choose the shogun from their own families for many generations. The Ashikaga family controlled the position for almost 235 years, then the Tokugawa family ruled for 264 years.

Until about 1867, Japan was run by a *feudal* system. It is the same type of government that the people of Europe

| A samurai warrior

used for many years after the fall of the Roman Empire. In a feudal system, the central government is not very strong. Hundreds or thousands of powerful men own large pieces of land and run them as if they were their own country.

These powerful **landlords**, called *daimyo* in Japan, kept their own private armies to defend their land. The soldiers in the private armies were called *samurai*. The samurai were fiercely loyal to their lord and lived by a strict **code** of behavior. The code required them to kill themselves if they ever broke it. The ordinary people had no power at all. They could not even own the land they farmed, and they had to obey the lords or risk being killed.

The Chinese tried to conquer Japan in the late 1200s. Twice they sent different fleets of ships with huge armies on board. Both times Japan was saved when the ships were driven back by sudden typhoons. The Japanese called the typhoons *kamikaze*, or "divine wind." They believed the typhoons showed that the gods were protecting their nation.

Beginning in about the 1600s, Europeans began to trade with China and eastern Asia. Many of the European nations conquered Asian nations or forced them to sign **treaties** that gave the Europeans many advantages in trading. The Japanese saw all this and decided to close their islands to outsiders.

A Catholic priest named Francis Xavier had been the first Christian missionary to Japan. He arrived in 1549. Many Japanese people became Christians in the years that followed, until the shogun decided to end contact with the outside. The shogun feared that the Christians would be disloyal, so most of them were killed. Only a very few survived. Quietly, for generations, they passed their faith down to a few others in secret.

| Japan hired Europeans to help them build a modern navy

The Japanese did not allow visitors for many years. They even killed sailors who were accidentally shipwrecked on their islands. Finally, the United States decided to force them to stop this policy. In 1853, a group of navy ships commanded by Commodore Matthew Perry sailed to Japan and insisted that the shogun sign a trade treaty. Faced with the power of the U.S. navy, the shogun agreed, and other trade treaties followed quickly.

The lords did not like the new treaties which were good for the foreigners, but not so good for the Japanese. The lords threw out the shogun and gave power back to the emperor in 1867. The new emperor took the name *Meiji*, which means "enlightened rule." The time he ruled is known as the Meiji Period. It was a time of great changes for Japan.

The Japanese did not want to become another European colony, so they began to learn western ways in order to use the knowledge to protect themselves. Europeans were hired to help the Japanese build a navy, an army, and industries. Japanese men were sent to modern nations to learn their ways and methods. Japan became a modern, industrial nation in one generation.

The Japanese quickly used their new power to conquer land around them. At the end of the 1800s, they had taken many of the islands near their homeland. By the early 1900s, Japan had an army in Korea. This led to the Russo-Japanese War in 1904 when the Russians, who also wanted Korea, tried to stop them. The Japanese stunned the European nations by defeating the Russians in battle. During World War I (1914 -1918), the Japanese took over German colonies in east Asia.

Match each word with the correct description.

3.20	_____ Meiji	a.	soldiers in a lord's army
3.21	_____ daimyo	b.	typhoon that ended Chinese attack
3.22	_____ samurai	c.	emperor's clan
3.23	_____ kamikaze	d.	system in Japan until 1867
3.24	_____ Yamato	e.	time of great changes for Japan
3.25	_____ shogun	f.	ruled in the emperor's name
3.26	_____ feudal	g.	landlords

Complete the following sentences.

3.27 The Japanese took much of their culture from the nation of _____ .

3.28 The Japanese believe their emperor was a descendent of the _____ goddess.

3.29 The first Christian missionary to reach Japan was a Catholic priest named _____ .

3.30 Japan defeated Russia in the _____ War of 1904.

3.31 During the Meiji Period the Japanese hired _____ to teach them how to build their industries and army.

3.32 After the Japanese saw the Europeans conquering land in Asia in the 1600s, they decided to stop all _____ between Japan and the outside world.

3.33 As soon as the Japanese had developed a modern country, they used their new power to _____ land around them.

3.34 American Commodore _____ forced the Japanese to begin contact with the outside world again in 1853.

After World War I, a new emperor, Hirohito, came to the throne. He quickly lost power as the soldiers took control of the government and began to conquer China. When World War II began in Europe in 1939, the Japanese became **allies** with the Germans and Italians. Japan took over French lands in east Asia after Germany conquered France in 1940.

The Japanese conquests worried the United States. America stopped all trade with Japan in 1941. Japan has so few natural resources, that it needed trade with the United States to get material for its industries. The soldiers in charge of the government decided that they would have to go to war with America and conquer Asia to get the resources they needed.

On December 7, 1941, the Japanese attacked the American navy base at Pearl Harbor in Hawaii. It was a sneak attack that destroyed eight battleships and killed over 2,000 American citizens. That brought the United States into World War II.

For several months the Japanese seemed to be unstoppable. They took the Philippines and much of southeast Asia in the early part of 1942. They were finally stopped just north of Australia in May of 1942 at the Battle of the Coral Sea. Then, in June of 1942, a large group of Japanese navy ships were defeated and several sunk at the Battle of Midway. The Japanese did not win a battle after that.

| Battle at Midway

Slowly the Americans captured the islands taken by the Japanese. With each victory, they got closer and closer to Japan. The Japanese continued to fight without surrender, according to their old samurai code. In August of 1945, the United States dropped **atomic bombs** on two Japanese cities, Hiroshima and Nagasaki. Both cities were destroyed, and thousands of people died. Japan surrendered, and the American army took over the country.

After World War II, most of Japan was in **ruins**. American General Douglas MacArthur, the military governor of Japan, worked to help the nation. He set up a new **democratic** government, and the United States helped rebuild Japanese industries. The emperor remained as the ruler, but he was not allowed to have any power. Instead the power of

| Atomic bomb exploding

the government was given to the *Diet*, the Japanese Congress. A new constitution gave the people the right to vote for their representatives and protected their freedom.

Japan's recovery from the destruction of the war was unbelievable. The only natural resource they had was their hard-working people. They rebuilt their industries using all the best and most modern equipment. Japan soon became one of the most productive nations on earth. By 1995, only the United States and China, both much larger nations, were producing more goods than Japan.

During the time the American army ran the nation, the land had been taken from the powerful lords and sold to the farmers who worked it. The last remains of the old feudal system were ended. All that remained was the emperor. He was still considered a god all the way through World War II. At the war's end, he admitted he was not a god. Emperor Hirohito lived until 1989. His son, Akihito, became the new emperor when his father died. Thus, Japan continues the 1,600-year-old custom of having an emperor from the Yamato clan.

Complete these sentences.

3.35 Emperor _____ came to the throne after World War I.

3.36 Japan was allied with the countries of _____ and _____

during World War II.

3.37 On December 7, 1941 Japan attacked the American base at _____

_____ in Hawaii.

3.38 After the Battle of _____ in June of 1942, Japan never won

another battle in World War II.

3.39 In August of 1945, America defeated Japan by dropping two

_____ on Japanese cities.

3.40 General _____ was the military governor of Japan after

World War II.

3.41 The Japanese Congress is called the _____ .

3.42 In 1995 only _____ and _____

produced more goods than Japan.

3.43 In 1989 Emperor _____ became the ruler of Japan.

Nippon

The people of Japan call their country
Nippon, which means "source of the sun."
Since Japan is east of Asia, it seemed to
be the place the sun came from every
morning as it rose. The Japanese flag
shows a red sun in the center of a white
background.

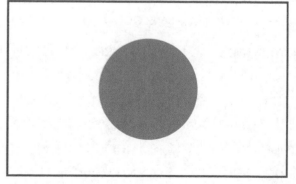

| Flag of Japan

Nippon today is a very unique place. The people have cars, televisions, video games, and movies, much like we do in the United States; but their culture, or way of life, is very different from America's. They think, eat, and live in their own ways.

Business. Japanese businesses are among the best in the world. They lead the world in making electronic equipment. Many of the video players, televisions, computers, video games, cameras, and video cameras in American homes were made in Japan. The Japanese also are important producers of cars, chemicals, and cloth.

Japan makes more goods than its own people can buy, and these are sold to other countries. Because they have so few natural resources, the Japanese must import all the materials they need to build their goods. Almost all of the oil, coal, or natural gas to run their factories also must come from another country. Thus, Japan has to trade with other nations for its industries to continue. To do this, they have the largest merchant fleet (ships that carry trade goods) in the world.

Japanese businesses want to make their product the very best in the world. They spend a large part of the money they make to improve their factories. Companies are always trying to build things better and faster.

Employees are encouraged to make suggestions and spot problems. Companies expect their people to work long hours and be loyal. Companies often have songs the employees sing together before they start work. People will usually work for the same company all their lives. Employees are rarely fired, even when their company is having trouble making money.

Japan is very crowded. Very little of the land is flat enough for people to live on or build businesses. The Japanese have built many fast trains to move all of the people from their homes to work each day. One kind of train is called the "Bullet Train" because of its speed. It moves all over Honshu at 130 miles per hour (210 km/hr), twice as fast as most cars. The trains are so crowded that special officials actually push to pack people onto the trains so that the door will shut!

| Bullet train

In spite of the lack of land for crops, the Japanese grow more than half of the food their people need. They do this by making very good use of the land they have. Farmers will often raise two or three crops every year on one piece of land. The most important crop is rice. Japanese people eat rice as often as Americans eat bread. It is their main food.

Second only to rice, the Japanese like to eat fish. They have never had much land to raise animals, so instead they get their meat from the sea. Fishing is, therefore, an important industry. Only boats from China and a few other countries catch more fish

| Sushi is a combination of rice and fish.

Write *true* or *false* on the blank.

3.44 _____ Japanese people call their country Nippon.

3.45 _____ Japan does not manufacture many goods.

3.46 _____ Japan leads the world in producing oil.

3.47 _____ Japan has the largest merchant fleet in the world.

3.48 _____ Japanese businessmen do not care about making their product well or quickly.

3.49 _____ Employees usually work for the same company all their lives.

3.50 _____ Japan is very crowded.

3.51 _____ Japanese people use trains to get to work.

3.52 _____ The most important Japanese food is chicken.

3.53 _____ Japanese people eat a lot of fish.

3.54 _____ Japanese fisherman catch more fish than any other country.

than the Japanese fishing fleet. In 2005 the Japanese caught 75 pounds (34 kg) of fish for every one in the country.

People. The Japanese people are very polite. They live in a crowded country and must get along with others. Japanese people greet each other by bowing. The more important the person you are meeting, the deeper the bow. Children bow to parents and teachers to greet them.

| Bowing is a greeting

Japanese are taught to work together much more than to be **independent**. Until very recently, Japanese children did not even have their own birthday. All of the children born during the year became a year older on New Year's Day! They were part of the group born that year.

Almost all of the people of Japan are from one race, have the same language, the same history, and the same religion. They are part of one big group. They do not like people to be different or unique. Japanese children are taught to do things together. They are taught to think in the same ways. When a decision must be made, all the people involved meet and come to an agreement.

Education is important to the Japanese. It is very difficult to read and write their language. Instead of a 26-letter alphabet such as we have, the Japanese language has 50,000 symbols that stand for different words. A person must learn close to 2,000 of them to read books and newspapers—but almost everyone in Japan can do it!

School is very hard work for Japanese children. A person's success as an adult is decided by the kind of education he gets. A person who gets into one of the best universities will always get a good job. To get into the best university, you first have to get into a good elementary school, junior high, and high school.

All the children take difficult tests in school to decide who gets into the better schools. Japanese children are pushed very hard by their parents to do well on the exams. A test taken when a child is ten may decide how good a job he has when he is forty! Many of the children go to special schools after school and on weekends to study for the tests. These are called *juku*, or cram schools. It is not unusual for the children to stay there until late in the evening.

Life. Houses are very small in Japan because there is so little land to use for building. It is very normal for a family's house to have three rooms and be just a little larger than a two car garage. If the family is lucky, they will also have a tiny space for a garden. These are jokingly referred to as being the size of a cat's forehead.

| Japanese family eating

The floor of the house is covered with straw mats called *tatami*. People never wear shoes in the house. They leave their shoes near the door and wear slippers inside. Families keep extra slippers for visitors.

Japanese houses also have no beds. There is no room for them. Instead everyone sleeps on the floor on thick quilts called *futons*. Every morning the futons are rolled up and put away in a closet or cabinet. Thus, the room can be used for a living room during the day and a bedroom at night.

Japanese people usually dress in clothes that are very much like the ones worn in America, but for special occasions both men and women will wear *kimonos*. Kimonos are long, beautiful, decorated robes tied with a wide sash. They are only worn for special occasions because they are very expensive. A woman's good kimono can cost thousands of dollars.

| Woman in a kimono

Write *true* or *false* on the blank.

3.55 _____ Japanese people are taught to be polite and be part of the group.

3.56 _____ Japanese people come from many different tribes.

3.57 _____ Most people can read and write in Japan.

3.58 _____ Japanese schools are easy and do not require much work.

3.59 _____ A *juku* is a Japanese book.

3.60 _____ Houses are usually large in Japan.

3.61 _____ Japanese people do not wear shoes in the house.

3.62 _____ Japanese people sleep on quilts on the floor.

3.63 _____ A kimono is a robe and sash worn on special occasions.

Religion. The Japanese follow two religions, Shinto and Buddhism. Shinto is older and is the national religion. Shinto means "the way of the gods." It has many, many gods, called *kami*. The kami are in everything in nature. In fact, Shinto teaches the importance of nature and the order of life.

People worship in the Shinto religion by leaving small gifts of food or flowers for the gods. They do not worry about life after death. They believe their spirits go to the mountains to live after they die. People often worship the spirits of their dead family members and give them offerings, too.

Torii gates are set up in front of Shinto **shrines**. These are two pillars connected above people's heads by a crossbar. The gates mark the separation of the real world from the spirit world.

Shinto has been influenced by Buddhism and Confucianism, religions from China. Shinto teaches people to live good lives, to work together, and to respect nature. Shinto recognizes that people sin. The gods are asked to help remove the sins and their bad results. Mostly, however, the gods are asked to help people get things or to bless and protect something.

| A Torii gate

A new car, for example, might be taken to a Shinto priest for a blessing.

Buddhism came to Japan about 1,500 years ago from China. Like most religions of eastern Asia, Buddhism does not claim to be the only true religion. People can be both Buddhist and Shinto, and many are.

Buddhism in Japan is adapted to the Japanese culture. There is little teaching about rebirth as something that happens after you die. (That is an important part of Buddhism in India and Nepal, where the main religion is Hinduism). Instead, Buddhism in Japan teaches people to seek peace inside themselves by **meditating**. Japanese Buddhists stress self-discipline and order. That fits well with Japanese people.

Only a very small number of people in Japan are Christians. Being a Christian makes Japanese people different, something they are taught to avoid.

Art. Japan is a beautiful country with big mountains, many swift rivers, deep bays, seaside beaches, and cliffs, as well as the nearby ocean. It is not surprising that Japanese religion and art have a lot to do with that beauty. Japanese people love natural, peaceful, orderly things.

No Japanese woman is thought to be properly educated until she knows the art of *ikebana*, flower arranging. The Japanese put just a few flowers in each bouquet. They want you to see each flower. Three blossoms are usually chosen—a tall flower, a short one, and a medium-sized one. The tallest flower points upward and stands for heaven. The shortest bends down toward earth. In between is the medium-length flower, representing mankind, the people who live on earth. The flowers are supposed to look as if they are still growing.

Bonsai is another form of living art. Bonsai trees are miniature trees, just a foot or less tall. They are grown in small dishes. A bonsai master will cut and wire the tree until it looks like an old tree on a sea cliff.

| A man trimming a bonsai tree

It must be constantly trimmed to stay small and correctly shaped. Often the trees are passed from parents to children, who continue to care for them.

The Japanese have many beautiful old crafts that are done by hand. Today the people who are good at these crafts are given the title "Living National Treasure." They are given money by the government so they can work at their craft and teach others about it. Some of the craftsmen hand-paint kimonos. Others make **pottery** by hand. Still others make dolls, play old musical instruments, or make carved boxes. Japanese love these carefully made things and give them places of honor in their homes.

Japanese people also like plays and movies. *Kabuki* plays use fancy costumes and makeup. All of the parts are played by men. The Japanese also have a type of play that is performed by puppets. The man who holds the puppet sits on the stage where the audience can see him. Japan makes many modern movies for theaters and television, too.

| Kabuki actor

Japanese writing is considered to be art as well. The many Japanese language symbols are painted with a brush to make them pretty to look at and read. This is called *calligraphy*. Children are taught it in school.

Japanese children are also taught how to write poetry in school. Poetry writing has been a sign of an educated person for many, many years in Japan. Even the old samurai warriors were expected to write good poetry.

One popular form of poetry is the *haiku*. A haiku has 17 syllables. It does not rhyme and often describes something beautiful in nature.

Block printing has been popular in Japan for hundreds of years. Artists would carve a picture on a wooden block and print it on a piece of paper. Often the artist would use different blocks for different colors, to make very realistic pictures of Japanese life.

The Japanese also make art out of folded paper. It is called *origami*. Pieces of paper are cleverly folded to look like birds or animals. Children learn origami in school, too.

The Japanese have even made a beautiful ceremony out of serving tea, their most popular drink. The tea ceremony is taught by tea masters all over Japan. It is a careful, step-by-step preparation and serving of tea to a special group of guests. It is meant to be peaceful and to display the special tea set used in the serving. Thus, the Japanese have many ways to find beauty and quiet in their busy, crowded land.

Match these words with the correct description.

3.64	_____ Shinto	a. flower arranging
3.65	_____ kami	b. art of folding paper
3.66	_____ Torii	c. beautiful writing
3.67	_____ Buddhism	d. a play with fancy costumes
3.68	_____ bonsai	e. poem with 17 syllables
3.69	_____ kabuki	f. gate for Shinto shrine
3.70	_____ haiku	g. national religion of Japan
3.71	_____ origami	h. religion that came from China teaching inner peace
3.72	_____ calligraphy	i. miniature trees
3.73	_____ ikebana	j. gods

Write true or false on the blank.

3.74 _____ Shinto has many gods.

3.75 _____ Buddhism teaches people to meditate to find peace inside themselves.

3.76 _____ Many beautiful crafts are done by Japan's Living National Treasures.

3.77 _____ Japanese people do not like poetry.

3.78 _____ The tea ceremony is a noisy party using loud musical instruments.

3.79   **Color this Japanese flag.**

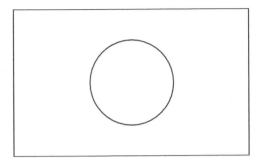

Make a picture display of Japanese manufacturers.

3.80   Look in your town's newspaper for Japanese advertisements.

a.   See if you can find any advertisements from car dealers who sell Japanese cars or motorcycles.

b.   See if you can find any ads for Japanese cameras.

c.   Look for advertisements of electric appliances such as computers, televisions, radios, media players, etc. Bring them to class and set up a picture display of Japanese manufacturers.

> ✓ **Teacher check:**
>
> Initials _____   Date _____

Before you take this last Self Test, you may want to do one or more of these self checks.

1.   _____   Read the objectives. See if you can do them.

2.   _____   Restudy the material related to any objectives that you cannot do.

3.   _____   Use the **SQ3R** study procedure to review the material:

a.   **S**can the sections.

b.   **Q**uestion yourself.

c.   **R**ead to answer your questions.

d.   **R**ecite the answers to yourself.

e.   **R**eview areas you did not understand.

4.   _____   Review all vocabulary, activities, and Self Tests, writing a correct answer for every wrong answer.

SELF TEST 3

Put a C in the blank if the statement is about Cuba, an I if it is about Iceland, or a J if it is about Japan (2 points each answer).

3.01 _____ in the Pacific Ocean

3.02 _____ near the Arctic Circle

3.03 _____ Honshu and Hokkaido

3.04 _____ Isle of Youth

3.05 _____ Communist government

3.06 _____ settled by Vikings

3.07 _____ touches the East China Sea

3.08 _____ Shinto and Buddhism are important religions

3.09 _____ part of Europe

3.010 _____ part of Asia

3.011 _____ dangers include typhoons, earthquakes, and tsunamis

3.012 _____ sugar is the most important export

3.013 _____ the shogun, daimyo, and samurai once were in power

3.014 _____ a leader in electronic equipment

3.015 _____ was ruled by Denmark

3.016 _____ favorite foods are rice and fish

3.017 _____ part of North America

3.018 _____ Westmann Islands

3.019 _____ part of the Antilles Islands

3.020 _____ sheep are the most important farm animal

Match these item (2 points each answer).

3.021	_____	Reykjavík	a.	capital of Japan
3.022	_____	Havana	b.	mountain in Japan
3.023	_____	Tokyo	c.	clan of the Japanese emperor
3.024	_____	Althing	d.	Icelandic parliament
3.025	_____	Kyushu	e.	Japanese parliament
3.026	_____	Fuji	f.	Shinto shrine gate
3.027	_____	Yamato	g.	"source of the sun"
3.028	_____	Diet	h.	capital of Cuba
3.029	_____	Nippon	i.	Japanese island
3.030	_____	Torii	j.	capital of Iceland

Complete these sentences using the words in the list (2 points each answer).

Korea	Greenland	Caribbean	Meiji	Bonsai
Origami	haiku	Skyr	tobacco	atoll

3.031 _____ is the land closest to Iceland.

3.032 The _____ was a ruler, and a time period named after him

brought great changes to Japan.

3.033 _____ is the art of creating beautiful animals out of folded

paper.

3.034 A _____ is a poem with 17 syllables.

3.035 _____ is the national dish of Iceland.

3.036 The _____ Sea is south of Cuba.

3.037 An _____ is a circle-shaped coral island with a lagoon in the center.

3.038 _____ is the land closest to Japan.

3.039 _____ trees are miniature trees shaped to look old and windblown.

3.040 The second most important crop in Cuba is _____ .

Write *true* or *false* on the blank (1 point each answer).

3.041 _____ The Sea of Okhotsk is north of Iceland.

3.042 _____ The Japanese Islands are mainly mountains.

3.043 _____ Japan had a feudal government before the 1800s

3.044 _____ Japan fought against the U.S. in World War II and won.

3.045 _____ Japanese schools are very difficult and children must work hard.

3.046 _____ Japan has a large amount of good farmland.

3.047 _____ Iceland's farmland is along the coast.

3.048 _____ Japan is a very crowded country.

3.049 _____ Goods are not usually made well in Cuba.

3.050 _____ The Shinto religion worships only one god.

3.051 _____ Japanese people love beauty in nature.

3.052 _____ Fidel Castro is the European who discovered Cuba.

3.053 _____ Cuba has fertile soil and good mineral resources.

3.054 _____ Houses are usually small in Japan.

3.055 _____ Volcanoes are common in Japan and Iceland.

3.056 _____ Cuba has a large amount of geothermal power.

3.057 _____ Fishing is an important industry in Iceland and Japan.

3.058 _____ Madagascar is the largest island in the West Indies.

3.059 _____ Indonesia has about 150 islands.

3.060 _____ Cuba is in the Indian Ocean.

Teacher check:

Score _____

Initials _____

Date _____

80 / 100

Before you take the LIFEPAC Test, you may want to do one or more of these self checks.

1. _____ Read the objectives. See if you can do them.

2. _____ Restudy the material related to any objectives that you cannot do.

3. _____ Use the **SQ3R** study procedure to review the material.

4. _____ Review activities, Self Tests, and LIFEPAC vocabulary words.

5. _____ Restudy areas of weakness indicated by the last Self Test.